What Are
Pulleys?

by Helen Frost

Consulting Editor: Gail Saunders-Smith, Ph.D.

Consultant: Philip W. Hammer, Ph.D.
Assistant Director of Education
American Institute of Physics

Pebble Books

an imprint of Capstone Press
Mankato, Minnesota

Pebble Books are published by Capstone Press
151 Good Counsel Drive, P.O. Box 669, Mankato, Minnesota 56002
www.capstonepress.com

3 4 5 6 7 8 11 10 09 08 07 06

Library of Congress Cataloging-in-Publication Data
Frost, Helen, 1949–
    What are pulleys? / by Helen Frost.
    p. cm.—(Looking at simple machines)
    Includes bibliographical references (p. 23) and index.
    ISBN 0-7368-0847-7 (hardcover)
    ISBN 0-7368-9138-2 (softcover)
    1. Pulleys—Juvenile literature. [1. Pulleys.] I.Title. II. Series.
TJ1103. .F76 2001
621.8′11—dc21

                                                            00-009870

Summary: Simple text and photographs present pulleys and their function as a
simple machine.

Note to Parents and Teachers

The Looking at Simple Machines series supports national science
standards for units on understanding work, force, and tools. This
book describes pulleys and illustrates how they make work easier.
The photographs support early readers in understanding the
text. This book also introduces early readers to subject-specific
vocabulary words, which are defined in the Words to Know section.
Early readers may need assistance to read some words and to use
the Table of Contents, Words to Know, Read More, Internet Sites,
and Index/Word List sections of the book.

Table of Contents

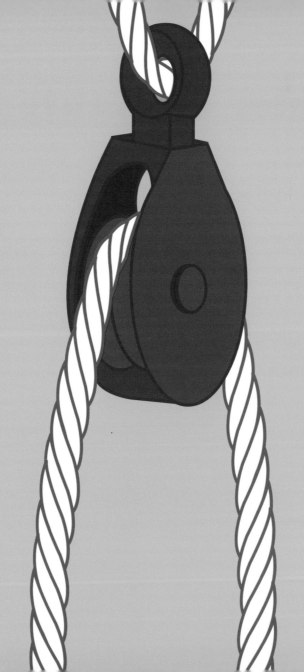

4

A pulley is
a simple machine.

wheel

A pulley has a wheel.

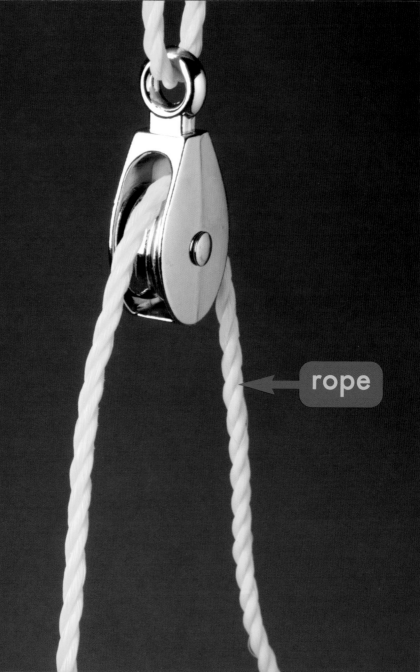

rope

A rope goes
around the wheel.

force

load

A load is attached to one end of the rope. A force pulls on the other end of the rope.

The pulley changes the direction of the force. The rope is pulled down and the load is pulled up.

pulley

A pulley makes lifting or moving a load easier.

pulley

People use pulleys
to raise and lower flags.

pulley

People use pulleys
to open and close blinds.

pulleys

People use pulleys
to lift heavy loads.

Words to Know

blind—a covering for a window; a pulley helps to open and close blinds.

direction—the way something is moving; up, down, right, and left are directions.

flag—a cloth with a pattern that is a symbol of a country or organization; a pulley helps to raise and lower a flag on a flagpole.

force—a push or a pull on an object; force makes objects start moving, speed up, change direction, or stop moving; a downward force on a pulley causes an object to move up.

pull—to move something toward you; it is easier to pull something than to push it; a pulley allows people to pull instead of push.

pulley—a rope around a wheel with a grooved rim; a pulley makes it easier to lift or move objects; a pulley is a simple machine.

simple machine—a tool that makes work easier; work is using a force to move an object across a distance.

Read More

Glover, David. *Pulleys and Gears.* Simple Machines. Crystal Lake, Ill.: Rigby Interactive Library, 1997.

Oxlade, Chris. *Machines.* Young Scientist Concepts and Projects. Milwaukee: Gareth Stevens, 1998.

Wells, Robert E. *How Do You Lift a Lion?* Morton Grove, Ill.: Albert Whitman, 1996.

Welsbacher, Anne. *Pulleys.* Understanding Simple Machines. Mankato, Minn.: Bridgestone Books, 2001.

Internet Sites

FactHound offers a safe, fun way to find Internet sites related to this book.

Go to *www.facthound.com*

He'll fetch the best sites for you!

Index/Word List

Word Count: 88
Early-Intervention Level: 12

Editorial Credits
Martha E. H. Rustad, editor; Kia Bielke, cover designer and illustrator; Kimberly
 Danger, photo researcher

Photo Credits
Capstone Press/CG Book Printers, cover, 6, 8
David F. Clobes, 10, 12, 16, 18
Photo Network/Larry Dunmire, 1
Visuals Unlimited/D. Yeske, 14; Jeff Greenberg, 20

The author thanks the children's section staff at the Allen County Public Library in
Fort Wayne, Indiana, for research assistance. The author also thanks Josué Njock Libii,
Ph.D., Associate Professor of Mechanical Engineering at Indiana University—Purdue
University.